D0685283

FALLING UP

A Memoir of Second Chances

FALLING UP

A Memoir of Second Chances

SCOTT EDWARD ANDERSON

THE LITTLE BOUND BOOKS ESSAY SERIES
WWW.LITTLEBOUNDBOOKS.COM

LITTLE BOUND BOOKS
Small Books. Big Impact | www.littleboundbooks.com

Quantity sales. Special discounts are available on quantity
purchases by corporations, associations, bookstores and others.
For details, contact the publisher or visit wholesalers such as
Ingram or Baker & Taylor.

The author has tried to recreate events, locales, and conversations
from his memories of them. In order to maintain their anonymity,
in some instances, he has changed the names of individuals and
places, he may have changed some identifying characteristics,
and details such as physical properties, occupations and places of
residence.

Published in 2019 • Little Bound Books
Imprint of Homebound Publications
Front Cover Image: Diane Stiglich, Ghost Bird, 2015. Acrylic
and charcoal on paper, 55" x 49". Private collection. Used by
permission of the artist. © 2015 by Diane Stiglich
Cover and Interior Designed • Leslie M. Browning
ISBN • 978-1-947003-48-4
First Edition Trade Paperback

10 9 8 7 6 5 4 3 2 1

Homebound Publications is committed to ecological stewardship.
We greatly value the natural environment and invest in
environmental conservation.

For Samantha, f, c & a,
and for
Jasper, Elizabeth, Walker
Max, Erica, and Sasha

———

———

1.

The Fall

"Steve Jobs is dead," I said.

A collective gasp went through the audience. We all knew he'd been sick—his seven-year battle with pancreatic cancer was well-covered by the media—still, the news of his death that morning was a shock. The Apple-founder, perhaps the most consequential tech CEO in history, had transformed our lives in so many ways and now he was dead. He was fifty-six years old. In that relatively short lifespan, he'd accomplished so much—arguably, many of us were at this conference, a gathering of some of the best and brightest from the worlds of technology, culture, and sustainability, because of his example. He'd touched so many, regardless of whether we used Apple products. Indeed, he had inspired a lot of people at the conference and around the globe to devote themselves to changing the world for the better.

Fifty-six. As I stood on the stage that October morning in 2011, a couple of years shy of fifty myself, I couldn't help thinking—as perhaps many in the room were thinking, too, in the wake of the example of Jobs—what have I done with my life? Have I lived up to my full potential? Have I done everything I could to make the world a better place? Isn't that why we're here? Not just here at this conference, billed as "three days to save the Earth," but on the planet itself. Perhaps everyone in the room, like me, weighed their achievements, their aspirations, and how they had lived their lives. And perhaps, like me, everyone wondered how they wanted to spend the rest of their time on the planet.

For me, the run-up to that October day had been a year of constant turmoil and self-torturing reflection. My thoughts and feelings ran riot in my mind, veering from a tormenting sense of failure and inadequacy to an inflated sense of self-worth and hubris, from a pessimistic view of my prospects to a belief in the abundance that would come my way through persistence. My career had been in a major upheaval over the previous four years as I pivoted from a decade and a half working in conservation onto a new path trying to establish myself in clean-tech and alternative energy. My marriage of nearly twenty years was on the verge of collapse—I'd been painfully unhappy for many years and was desperate to leave, but with three kids under the age of sixteen, I felt paralyzed by the potential impact leaving would have on them. As if that wasn't enough, I'd fallen in love outside of marriage and felt compelled to seize the opportunity offered by this new relationship or risk losing what I saw as the chance of a lifetime—a last chance at happiness and authentic, uncompromised love.

Jobs's death struck a chord—he was such an un-compromising, disruptive, and creative person—a genius—always remaining true to himself and to his vision. Had I been true to my dreams? Had I lived my most authentic, purposeful life? If not, what was I waiting for? Life is short, I thought, and if I couldn't take the leap now, would I ever?

In truth, I was about to take the most radical leap of my life. I'd reached a turning point from which there was no going back, and this leap would impact my family, my friends, my livelihood—every aspect of my life. It was the culmination of several years of flux and turmoil, starting with my departure from the Nature Conservancy, one of the world's most successful conservation organizations, in 2007.

I left the Conservancy after fifteen years and embarked on what became a series of career pivots that led me through Ashoka, a kind of social venture capital organization that invests in entrepreneurs who are tackling some of the world's most pressing problems, and then to start my own venture, a web marketplace for green energy investing that became the victim of the financial market collapse of 2008-2009. Because I had done a lot of due diligence on companies for the marketplace, I was able to pivot that business idea into a consultancy advising clean-tech startups. This, in turn, led to my working with a sustainability centered bank that a client was trying to launch and into which I had thrown myself completely for much of 2011.

The idea had captured my imagination: build the country's first bank with environmental, societal, and financial concerns at its core. Moreover, it felt like a good way to repair the economy, being part of something that could help get green buildings built and environmentally friendly businesses off the ground. The only thing standing in our way was a bank charter, a critical document authorizing banking operations; not an easy thing to obtain in the wake of a banking crisis. The principals of the bank had applied for a "de novo" charter, essentially permission to establish a new bank, but their meetings were unsuccessful; the Fed decided there would be no new charters until the crisis was completely over. This held everything up for months, until finally, the Feds suggested my clients buy an existing bank charter from one of the hundreds of banks that were failing as a result of the mortgage-backed securities scandal that had, in part, triggered the collapse.

Truth be told, it wasn't easy to find a bank with a clean balance sheet and relatively solid foundation, but they'd zeroed in on one: a small community bank without a lot of bad loans, minimal infrastructure, and a good stable of existing customers. They had only a few months to raise the capital to obtain the charter and all the bank's assets. The principals had hired me to help them raise the money and we had talked about a potential role for me with the bank after the launch.

For much of the year leading up to this day, I'd been almost exclusively focused on helping them with their capital raise. I'd blown through my savings and investments and ran up some credit card debt to fund my work while building my own business over the past few years and the potential opportunity to be part of the team once the bank launched seemed like a path toward my own financial recovery. But time was running out. The bank we targeted burned through cash at an alarming rate, and the Feds were closing in, preparing to break up the bank and disperse its assets.

The clock was ticking. Our fundraising was going well, but needed to accelerate if we were going to reach the goal before the target bank failed. On the day before I left for Austin, we'd learned that the bank was in worse shape than we'd anticipated. Now, it looked like the deal wasn't going to happen. What was I going to do if it didn't come together? And if the bank didn't get launched, how would I be able to make the leap I needed to save myself?

My talk on that morning in Austin was part of the first South by Southwest Eco Conference, the sustainability arm of the renowned music and culture festival. Amidst all the anxiety, SXSW Eco promised 72 hours dedicated to green businesses, social enterprises, and environmental solutions. The event's focus provided a hopeful note in what had been a rough few years for everyone. The organizers had invited me to speak, in part, because of my work as a green consultant, advising cleantech companies and environmental organizations, as well as my recent work with the sustainability bank. I was speaking on the topic of reimagining financial services.

In the wake of this emotional tsunami, I felt dispirited and, frankly, a bit like a fraud. Who was I to talk about reimagining financial services when I was on the brink of failing in my attempt to do just that? As I looked out over the audience, however, I sensed that every face in the room looked as anxious about the future as I felt, they were eager for any hope or inspiration I could offer. Many of us were still reeling from the effects of the economic disaster of the past few years—I'd seen it with friends and colleagues, some of whom had lost everything, others were still struggling to get back on their feet. In my own life, I still felt a bit shell-shocked, like I was walking through a war zone, tiptoeing around mines, unexploded ordnance, and the detritus and fallout from one of the worst financial crises in history. We were—all of us—challenged by the new, uncharted world we were living in, a world for which we didn't have a compass to navigate let alone a map.

I led the audience in a moment of silence for Steve Jobs.

Then I remembered a story from my adolescence that had helped me navigate difficult situations throughout my life, a story that had become a kind of defining story for me, and that might have some relevance to the audience and what many of us were feeling.

*   *   *   *   *

When I was fifteen years old, I went hiking along Letchworth Gorge in upstate New York. Some areas of the gorge reach a vertical drop of 550 feet down to the Genesee River—all sandstone, siltstone, and shale. You'd think the fact that dozens of fatalities had occurred there over the years would have kept me from the edge, but I was fifteen and full of hubris. I got too close to the edge—and I fell.

I'm not sure how far I fell or for how long; it seemed like a long way and a long time, but it was likely just a matter of seconds. Time dragged, however, like a cartoon character falling off a cliff—think of Bugs Bunny falling, eating a carrot, reading *War & Peace*, and filing his nails. While falling, I felt oddly calm, at peace: one with the fall.

This was my first "Zen" moment. I gave into whatever was about to happen to me: whether dashed to the bottom of the gorge in a tangled, tortured mess; lifted by spirits and carried into the sky on a ribbon of sunlight; or somehow becoming one with the collective unconscious I'd begun to learn about from my adolescent fascination with Carl Jung, the Transcendentalists, and Transcendental Meditation. Whatever happened, I was fine with it. Totally fine with it. Almost I wanted to cross my arms over my chest, but I couldn't. Instead, they lifted above me like I was giving myself to the gorge.

And then it was over. My arm caught a branch or an exposed root. A jerking feeling like a parachute opening. I was safe. I fell, but I wasn't dead. After a few seconds of stunned silence, I climbed back up to the top of the gorge, loose shale wall crumbling below me with every inch up. Adrenalin got me up the shale face, nothing else. Once at the top of the gorge rim, I was calm; bewildered, but calm. I got a second chance.

*   *   *   *   *

Everyone has a defining story in their life, a story that helps us navigate our world, and put meaning into how we survive and move forward. For me, it was this story of my fall in the gorge and its aftermath—the second chance it gave me and the sense that I could overcome any set-back.

For Steve Jobs, I told the audience, it was his story about stumbling into a calligraphy class at Reed College after he'd dropped out of school. Inadvertently, that class led to Jobs creating multiple fonts for the Mac, thereby transforming personal computing. At the time, he couldn't know the influence that one class would have on his life and his work—indeed, on all our work. If he had never found that class, I shared with the audience in Austin, the computer revolution may have taken a completely different turn altogether. Jobs couldn't anticipate the impact that one class would have on him as he entered it, he was just following his gut—it looked like an interesting class. Later, he realized "you can't connect the dots going forward; you can only connect them looking backward." And, as Jobs related in his famous 2005 commencement speech at Stanford, "You have to trust that the dots will somehow connect in your future. You have to trust in something—your gut, destiny, life, karma, whatever." That was the message I tried to leave with the crowd in Austin in pairing these two stories. In this time of free-falling, I offered, we have a second chance to make the most of our lives, to look for unusual opportunities, to create the future we want out of the chaos we feel.

2.

LATE BLOOMER

WHAT DID I MAKE OF MY FIRST second chance after the fall? And what could it tell me about the life ahead of me and the choices I needed to make now?

For as long as I could remember, I wanted to be a poet, a writer. Like many teenagers who aspired to be writers and artists in the late 1970s, I romanticized the rebel genius. Some of my rebel heroes, Bob Dylan, Patti Smith, and Allen Ginsberg had sung the praises of Arthur Rimbaud, the visionary 19th Century French poet. So, I read Rimbaud.

What Rimbaud articulated, at age sixteen, found deep resonance with me around the same age, that the poet should be a visionary, a "seer." How do you do that? I wanted desperately to know.

In his "Lettre du Voyant" (Letter of the Seer), Rimbaud explained, "The poet makes himself a seer by a long, prodigious, and rational disordering of all the senses. Every form of love, or suffering, of madness; he searches himself, he consumes all the poisons in him, and keeps only their quintessences."

Rimbaud was a classic young literary success story: discovered in his teens, celebrated by the literati of his time, some of whom—literally—fell in love with him; one of whom shot him in a passionate fit of pique. Almost as quickly as he ascended, however, Rimbaud burned out. Fame and adulation weren't worth the price of his vision. He gave up poetry by the age of twenty-one, left Paris, became a soldier in the Dutch Colonial Army and traveled to Indonesia, only to desert and return to France, eventually landing in Yemen and Ethiopia, where he dealt in coffee and guns. He became a legend. His works are still read today. Rimbaud's poems seemed fully formed when they hit the page. Rimbaud was a genius. But after giving up poetry, he never wrote again.

*　　*　　*　　*　　*

When I became serious about writing poetry and making art around the age of fifteen, just after I fell at Letchworth Gorge, Rimbaud was one of the poets I read with passion, and my teenage poems were a mongrel-mix of French symbolism, New England transcendentalism, and Beat-generation rawness. In my mind, it was only a matter of time before I was "discovered" for my genius.

Genius or hubris? I did whatever I wanted as a young artist. I saw no limits or limitations for myself. At sixteen, I created a conceptual art space called "Arsenic Basement," in the cellar of my mother's house. A year later, I wrote a long poem on a single roll of adding machine tape, in emulation of another one of my adolescent heroes, Jack Kerouac, and his famous typescript for *On the Road*. "Burroughs Adding Machine Tape Roll Pome," I called it, liking the double play on the adding machine-maker Burroughs Corporation and Kerouac's pal, the writer William Burroughs. Composing a section every day, I fed the tape into my typewriter until I finished the roll.

In my mind, I wasn't just a genius with words. To me, everything I touched bore the marks of brilliance. Using a small, portable cassette player, I made recordings of experimental, atmospheric music in pale imitation of Brian Eno and Laurie Anderson. Meticulously filling journals for posterity, I captured my every thought, convinced of my imminent discovery and future fame—someday, the world would want to read my every word as a young poet and artist.

Before my nineteenth birthday, I launched a magazine called *Rockstop,* which I used to publicize my band, Active Driveway, with whom I performed as the pseudonymous lead singer and bass player, Dash Beatcomber. New York-area college radio stations regularly played our song, "Gotta Dance (Dance It Away)," in 1982. I even appeared in a commercial for the nascent cable music channel MTV, an ad for a line of logo-branded clothing they were promoting. And somewhere there's a local TV news interview from the mid-1980s with me in Cleveland, Ohio, where the magazine really took off—three minutes of my fifteen minutes of fame—in which I told the interviewer, "My life is my art."

Back then, my life was my art. I tried everything: painting, collages, assemblages, and short, mostly black & white *Super 8* films. A few of my works got shown in galleries from Kent State University to New

York. I even had a "one-man show" in Lakewood, Ohio, in 1986—albeit, in a booth I rented at an art-focused street fair.

I also experimented with other forms of art: there was an "earthwork," wherein I moved a pile of dirt from one location to another, documenting the entire process; an installation in a field behind a friend's upstate farmhouse constructed from discarded plumbing fixtures and farm machinery; and a multi-media performance piece at Gallery 53/ Smithy Artworks in Cooperstown, New York, featuring a mime, a mask of Jacques Cousteau's face on a stick, and Harry Belafonte recordings in a surrealistic dream-of-consciousness monologue poem.

In support of my art over that decade, I took several jobs: working as a baker's apprentice in a natural foods market; hand painting silk for a design company that supplied fashion designers like Mary McFadden, Calvin Klein, and Ralph Lauren; and managing print shops, which gave me access to presses and copiers I used for both my magazine and, later, for my self-published chapbooks of poetry.

For most of my life, I've had an entrepreneurial streak that made me both adaptable and inventive when it came to my survival. As a young boy, I'd created a lending library of my books, complete with an elaborate system for sign-outs. I had the usual paper routes and lawn cutting services that suburban youth once used to make pocket money. And in high school, I'd financed a trip to New York City by raising all the money I needed from friends and classmates.

Towards the end of the 1980s, I moved to Germany and Paris, where I wrote a book about another rebel-genius hero of mine, Marcel Duchamp, who had single-handedly disrupted modern art in the 20th Century by famously submitting an upturned urinal to an art exhibit. Returning to the States, I landed a job in publishing with an international literary agency, largely on the fact that I'd lived in Europe, spoke a bit of French and German, and had published my own magazine. A couple of years later, I joined the editorial team at the publishing house Viking Penguin.

Packaging several sections of my unfinished Duchamp book for the artist's centenary, I tried selling copies on the steps of the Philadelphia Museum of Art. When nothing sold, I told myself Duchamp would have appreciated the irony and gave a copy to an assistant of the museum director. At the decade's end, I became part of the Hoboken poetry scene at Maxwell's and Café Elysian and started a writing group with a few friends; we called ourselves the "Decompositionalists"—our work was decomposing rather than composing, like the society around us.

Looking back, I realize, I was not a genius. The common denominator of the work I produced back then? It sucked. Neither genius nor savant, it became clear I wasn't going to be discovered by a patron and rocketed to fame and fortune. But perhaps I didn't need to be a genius. Perhaps I didn't need to be Rimbaud. Unlike Rimbaud, I kept writing well into my twenties. In fact, as I grew older, I gave up everything—music, painting, filmmaking—except writing.

Approaching my thirties, I settled into a job with the Nature Conservancy, with whom I worked for the next fifteen years. That work informed my writing in ways I couldn't imagine and tapped into my boyhood passion for nature and the outdoors. This influence was not only evident in my poetry, for I wrote a book exploring natural history hikes in New York State, *Walks in Nature's Empire*, which was published in 1995. The Millay Colony for the Arts in Austerlitz, New York, gave me a residency in November of 2002, an entire month to focus on my writing. There I wrote my book, *Dwelling: an ecopoem*. A couple years later, I started a blog, *The Green Skeptic*, which I wrote for ten years, and landed on Fox Business as a green commentator with Varney & Company. For twenty-five years, I kept writing and revising, writing more and revising more, finally becoming, if not a "seer," becoming a poet, a writer.

The boy who didn't become Rimbaud and wasn't a genius, continued to apply and develop his skills, honing his craft. Connecting the dots over my life, I saw that my path had led me to a deeper dedication to two things I originally loved: nature and poetry. And it wasn't until just prior to my fiftieth birthday that I published my first full-length collection of poems, *Fallow Field*. It took me twenty-five years to complete that book, that's how far back a few of the poems were originated.

I once read an article by Malcolm Gladwell in *The New Yorker* called "Late Bloomers." He was writing about experimental innovators, building on a theory of artistic creativity first proposed by the economist

David Galenson in his 2007 book, *Old Masters and Young Geniuses: The Two Life Cycles of Artistic Creativity.* In that book, Galenson divided artists into two categories: "conceptualists," those who create their most important innovations at an early age, say, later teens or twenties, and "experimentalists," those whose innovations develop slowly over a long period of time, refined through constant experimentation. Conceptualists were young geniuses; experimentalists, late bloomers.

Today, I admit I'm no genius. Yet, after half a lifetime or more of writing and exploring by doing, I'm still blooming. Consequently, my writing improves the more I work at it or, at least, I hope so. I remain dedicated to craft and continue trying, keep experimenting, and striving to get better. I'm a late bloomer.

3.

THE LIFE YOU CHOOSE
MUST BE YOUR OWN

ABOUT THE TIME I WAS ADDRESSING that audience at
SXSW ECO in October 2011, I was in the middle of
what people call a mid-life crisis. I desperately need-
ed a change, another second chance. The disruption
I felt in my career was also being felt in my marriage.
Married almost twenty years, I had three kids, a
house, a dog, seemingly everything one could want.
But something inside me was deeply dissatisfied and
I had felt that way for years.

It wasn't just leaving the conservation work I
loved four years before to set out on new, uncharted
territory or the fact that the financial collapse had
sabotaged my dreams of creating something on my

own, or the sustainability bank deal that was falling apart. Truth is, I was a mess, leading a double life that was tearing me up inside and putting me in real danger. Moreover, I was deeply divided, scared, and not sure how I would survive.

Yet, there was also a ray of hope—a lifeline thrown to me in the form of a new relationship that helped me put my life in perspective, that helped me see the potential ahead of me, if only I was willing to fall up again.

Samantha worked for the Skoll Foundation, which supports social entrepreneurship, and a few years before she had invited me to speak at their annual forum in the spring of 2008. I had a prior commitment and couldn't attend, but we stayed in touch and our friendship grew organically over time, aided by the new social media technologies. As our relationship blossomed, we revealed how we were each miserable in our crumbling marriages and, as our friendship deepened, our conversations turned to commiseration and consolation.

We met for the first time in 2009, at 30th Street Station in Philadelphia, after I noticed her tweet that she and a colleague were having meetings in the city. "You can't be in my 'hood and not meet with me," I tweeted in response. So, I joined Samantha and her colleague for lunch in the train station, and we immediately hit it off. Several months later, when she moved back to the States, we started seeing each other regularly and, eventually, we both began to wonder what it would be like to be together, which would mean untangling from our failing marriages and managing the expectations of our kids. (She had three of her own.)

For most of my adult life, I had built up defenses to protect myself from getting close to people. My heart was broken in an early relationship in my twenties and I vowed never to let it happen to me again. The instinct to wall myself off from others caused me to appear aloof at times and prevented me from being fully invested in any relationship—with lovers, friends, co-workers, even my wife of nearly twenty years, the mother to my children.

In truth, I had come across as callous, cavalier, and uncaring. For as long as I could remember, my mother had called me intense; many of my friends felt they'd never really known me. For many years,

I'd lived a secret life, including several casual affairs, looking for love in all the wrong places, affairs that always ended because I couldn't or wouldn't let anyone in. It was a way to survive, but no way to live.

Now there was a crack in my armor. I could be myself with Samantha and she saw the best in me, somehow penetrating my shell. She, too, appeared to appreciate that I seemed to understand who she wanted to be in the world.

My guard was coming down fast and it scared me. Could I really allow myself to be that vulnerable with another person? We both wanted to go after everything we believed in, everything we desired— to be fully open to the experience of living. And it seemed like we could do that together.

*　　*　　*　　*　　*

After the conference, I was working with a career coach, Phyllis Mufson of Catalyst for Growth. In one exercise, Phyllis had me draw a circle on a piece of paper. "Close your eyes and imagine yourself standing in the middle of the circle," she said, which I did. "Now, think about the person you trust the most and invite that person into the circle with you. Who is it?"

I wasn't thinking about my children or any of my closest friends or colleagues, not even my wife. It was Samantha who came immediately to mind. I hadn't said anything to Phyllis about Samantha, but there she was, in my mind's eye, standing right next to me in the circle of my life.

In our next session, Phyllis asked me to close my eyes again and let myself drift. Her voice was soothing and hypnotic. I felt atypically safe and calm.

"Now, I want you to think of the future place where you'll live," she instructed. "And describe to me what you see."

Before me, I saw a curving stone path, densely surrounded by green foliage and multicolored flowers. It appeared to be tropical or sub-tropical. The path wound its way to a gate. The gate opened, and the path continued. More flowers and a rich, garden-like feeling. I knocked on the door.

"Who greets you at the door? Phyllis asked.

"A man. A man with a beard," I answered. "He seems very happy to see me. 'At last, you've arrived,' he says to me."

"Who is the man?" asked Phyllis.

"I think...I think it's me," I said. He welcomed me into his home, a neatly appointed house, lived-in, cozy. It felt warm, inviting. I felt at home. The man gave me a big bear hug.

"What's his name?" Phyllis asked.

"Papa," I said without hesitation. "He wants me to call him Papa. Papa is what my kids call me, a term of endearment, as well as, for me, a way to distinguish myself from my father, who was called 'Dad.' Dad never suited me. Papa is me."

And there was Papa—me or the future me—greeting me and welcoming me into his home, my future home. Welcoming me home. The encounter brought me to tears, overwhelmed by the power of the experience and moved by his presence. My presence; the future me.

Asked to describe him further, after coming out of the visualization, I used words like "gentle," "tender," "strong," "welcoming," "creative," "someone I want to be around." All those words described different aspects of me, only I'd masked some of them for too long. In trying to make myself invulnerable, I'd covered up so much of what made me a strong and purposeful man. In trying to protect myself, I'd built up calluses on my psyche; calluses that made me, well, callous; so unlike this man I met for the first time—the man I could become.

Still, there was a huge gap between the man I met in the garden house and the man sitting in Phyllis's office, meeting his potential future self—and we would spend our next several sessions focusing on bridging that gap.

*　　*　　*　　*　　*

"I want you to imagine yourself at the top of your game," Phyllis said to me at the beginning of our next session. I closed my eyes. "Tell me what you see, what you're doing, and what impact you're having on the people around you."

"I'm in a room, a big hall, it's filled with people, an audience," I ventured. "I'm giving a speech or a lecture or a talk. I can't make out what I'm saying, but the audience is clearly moved by it."

"What do you say that moves them," Phyllis asked. "What are they doing?"

"They're drawing closer together and to me on the stage," I answered. "I am bringing them together with my words."

That I was on stage wasn't surprising. Whether reading poetry or appearing on TV as a green pundit, give me a microphone and an audience and I'm happy. I thrive on public speaking in ways that others enjoy physical exercise: I get into a zone like athletes when they are pushing themselves. What surprised me in the exercise was to see so clearly that the person on stage was "Papa"—it was me as Papa—and I seemed to be bringing people together, influencing their thinking, giving them a new perspective.

Being at the top of my game, as Papa was in my visualization, clearly required my being in front of people, using my words, stories, and poetry to bring them together into some collective of individual actions that perhaps could change the world. Through this work with Phyllis, I was able to envision a new path for myself: a way of being in the world that had allowed me to be the man who pivoted in front of that audience in Austin to talk about what mattered most.

I realize now, I was projecting myself into that place, into that role, where I found strength in vulnerability. And where, finally, I could let down my guard, which would also give me a second chance in a relationship, with Samantha, where I could finally be fully open to the experience of being in love. In integrating the various strands of my life and who I am, I could also envision the kind of father I wanted to be, even if it meant a more complicated living arrangement. By being truly myself, I could demonstrate a path for my children as well, a path that led to an authentic place. It was really a chance to fulfill my dream of being who I wanted to be in the world. I was staring at another second chance.

4.

THE GIFT

OF A LIFETIME

ON THE DAY I TURNED FIFTY YEARS OLD, in November 2013, I went hiking with my three kids in Philadelphia's Wissahickon Valley Park, a wooded, 1,800-acre gorge with some 57 miles of trails. My oldest son, Jasper, then seventeen, had a spring in his step, enjoying the scenery, the fresh air, and being out in the woods. It had been awhile since we'd all been for a walk in the woods together. The twins, his younger siblings, were also getting excited in ways I hadn't seen before. Walker, my boy twin, stopped at the stump of a fallen tree cut to clear the trail. Counting the rings, he informed us the tree was likely 130 years old. His twin sister Elizabeth scrambled up the side of a craggy hill, proudly staking claim to part of it. A bald eagle flew over Wissahickon Creek. None of us said a word.

Deep down, I realized there was nothing better than this moment—I was truly happy out in the woods with my kids, for the first time in a long while, a couple of years since their mother and I broke up. The interval was a rough time, but we'd made it. Samantha and I got engaged in May of that year and were to be married the following spring. Her kids and mine had met over a camping trip the previous summer and had hit it off right away. Now, I saw that many of my concerns about my kids were unfounded; they were better off with "Papa"—the real, authentic me, who was finally fully available to them.

There, in the woods, as I saw their senses being aroused, their awareness of the world coming alive, their self-confidence building, I felt assured that our connection, our bond would grow through experiences like this together. This was a legacy of connectedness to nature that I had forged in my own childhood, through my own experiences in the natural world.

*   *   *   *   *

I often wandered alone in the woods at the ages of nine and ten years old. We lived in Plainville, Massachusetts, a typical, small sub-rural town between Providence and Boston, with a classic main street running through it, surrounded by woods, wetlands, and pastures.

One day, walking back from a friend's house, I took a detour through the woods, where I stumbled into a boggy wetland—probably around Fuller Pond, as I map it now. As soon as I stepped in, I realized my mistake. The mud grabbed my foot and held it tight. Somehow, I knew not to panic. When I put my other foot on solid ground and started to pull out my stuck foot, I felt my sneaker getting pulled off by the mud and pushed down slightly until my foot slipped back into my sneaker, then tried again, with the same result. Finally, on my third try, out came my foot and sneaker intact.

Twenty years later, while working for the Nature Conservancy in New York's Hudson Valley, I found myself in that same kind of wetland habitat. Even if

I didn't know the names, I recognized some of the same plants and conditions from back in Plainville. I built upon my childhood experience and this time, as an adult, I knew where not to step—unless wearing mud boots.

*   *   *   *   *

The fact is, my son Jasper had long been developing his own connectedness to nature, simply by growing up in proximity to the natural world, and he seemed to be enthusiastic about learning from his surroundings.

Like most toddlers, Jasper first experienced the world by jumping, running, rushing, and flinging himself into it. Born in Anchorage, Alaska, Jasper's first playground—our backyard—was the Chugach Mountains that surround the city. He enjoyed the view from the backpack-child carrier for a while, but as soon as he could walk, he wanted to get out and *move*. I'd set him down and the tiny engines in his kid-size lightweight hiking boots got moving—*fast*. He clambered into the blueberry bushes on the hillside. He giggled, looking up at me, wanting me to react. Falling butt-first into the berries, he laughed like a berry-mad bear, reminding me of the playful black bear cub we saw a few weeks before at the Alaska Zoo, pacing back and forth, climbing and tumbling over logs and berry bushes in the habitat created for it by the zoo staff. From then on, Jasper's nickname was "Little Bear" to my "Papa Bear."

When Jasper pitched forward out of the blueberries and down onto the gravel and dirt path, I resisted the urge to rescue him. At the precise moment before impact, he tucked under and rolled off the trail and onto the soft tundra. How did he know how to do this? His rolling left him berry-stained, a little dusty, and very pleased with himself.

Back in the pack, Jasper rode up to the first of two low summits. Suddenly, from below us, we heard the others in our party. They'd spotted a porcupine lumbering up a narrow, shallow ravine. Jasper couldn't see it from that distance, but neither was he concerned. He got bored with standing in one spot, kicked at my back, and shouted, "Go! Go!"

We headed for the top of the second summit, Jasper humming happily in my ear. I fed him blueberries over my shoulder. Not enough of the berries were as ripe as we'd want if we were collecting bushels, but some were sweet enough to please this toddler and his papa. Slapping me with joy, he smeared blueberry juice in my hair and all over my neck. I couldn't see his face, but I knew there was a big, purple smile behind me.

If moments like this have any lasting effect, I suspect they engender a connectedness to the land through memory, which creates a sense of place. Someday, Jasper may feel an inexplicable pull to seek out experiences such as this on his own and with his own children, who will teach him to see nature with fresh eyes, as Jasper showed me. A child gives a parent the gift of slowing down and seeing the world anew.

My son slowed me down on trails and in the backyard, where he had his favorite birch tree, among the flowers, moss, and mushrooms. Slowing down, I looked more closely at the little things surrounding us. Jasper picked up a leaf, showed it to me. "Leaf," I said. He tried to mimic me, but there were too many "efs" in his version of the word. Still, I responded, "Yes, that's it: LEAFFFF." Learning more about the natural world by observing what he observed;

lingering over the objects he lingered over, I paid close attention for another reason: I wanted him to know what these things are one day, when naming things became important to him. I loved discovering *with* him, but I also wanted to have the answers to his questions when they came down the trail.

*   *   *   *   *

A few years later, we moved to Philadelphia for my work and began learning a different habitat. In our backyard, we concentrated on one small square of property—our backyard—which we sectioned off into separate areas. Each area had its own collection of flora and fauna—whether it was tomatoes and vegetables (and the occasional woodchuck) in the garden or the flower beds I painstakingly transformed to species native to Pennsylvania and divided into woodland, grassland, and wildflower habitats. By this time, my twins had also arrived and we spent hours together in the garden and in the woods along Wissahickon Creek.

In the end, this approach to studying nature—through small-scale exploration and paying attention—paid off. And I needed no further evidence than our walk in the Wissahickon on my fiftieth, my excitement growing along with theirs. Being out in nature is a gift that goes beyond a birthday; it is the gift of a lifetime.

5.

TELLING STORIES TO CHANGE THE WORLD

MY CHILDREN HAVE ALWAYS LOVED STORIES. When Jasper was little, I told stories to him every night at bedtime. He came to rely on these stories to fall asleep each night and, to entertain him and me, I needed to become more and more creative with each telling. Soon the stories had recurring characters, including his stuffed bear, "Babe."

The stories he liked best were about Babe getting lost. Particularly, things that really happened to Babe: Babe getting left behind in a blueberry patch, on a hike in Alaska's Chugach Mountains, or in the Kauai Airport on vacation. The stories would always end with Babe being safe, found, or delivered back into Jasper's arms by me or by a Good Samaritan. The message, I realize now, was that the world was a safe and nurturing place for Babe—and for Jasper.

My twins, seven years his junior, continued their brother's love of story. In fact, during a camping trip when they were three, they started telling their own stories, featuring themselves as the heroes or protagonists. The stories all had the same basic plot and started, "Walking in a forest we come across a little bear. The bear says to us, 'I'm lost, and I need to find my home.'" After which the twins would each take turns telling the bear how to get there, until finally one of them would pronounce that the bear was already home and now it was time for the twins to return home. "That is all the story," one of them would always say. "Good night, Papa."

I have seen how stories build worlds and define worldviews. From the time we first hear and tell them, stories help us face our fears, express our dreams, and share our beliefs and values with others. Through stories we can truly change the world for the better.

Stories about change are narratives of conflict and hope, problems and solutions. A conflict of some kind is set up that leads the reader to hope. Telling these stories helps others make change, empowering them, and inspiring them to act. Through storytelling, people "form the belief that it is possible to make the world a better place," says journalist David Bornstein. "Those who act on that belief spread it to others," sparking social movements and change.

When I worked as a fundraiser in conservation, our stories tended to be about "bucks and acres"—if you give us a million dollars, you can help us protect so many acres or save a species. We focused on how much land we protected, the species we saved, and how much money it took to do the deal.

Too often, we left out the back story of the human beings and communities affected by our work. These stories were about the families and individuals who lived, worked, and depended on the land and waters for economic and spiritual sustenance. The back stories were much more compelling than any bucks and acres narrative. More persuasive stories lingered in the back story, and telling those stories resonated with people, turning the conservation transaction into a powerful and persuasive narrative of transformation. A story about a family that faced the loss of their farm, for example, a farm that had been in their family for generations, and where, because they had been such good stewards over the years, the land also supported habitat for rare turtles, was more compelling than a story about buying 140 acres for a certain cash value.

If we are going to build a conservation ethic and change the world, we need to share our stories of hope and nurture a culture of storytelling. We need to get at the heart of what makes conservation relevant and important to people for the future of our species.

I firmly believe that we're on the cusp of a great potential transformation, becoming the change we want to effect, sharing our stories full of hope and possibility. I want to be a part of that story and I want my kids to be part of that story too.

6.

FALLING UP

BEFORE I SAT DOWN TO WRITE this memoir, I saw my life and career path as one of constant zigging and zagging through a series of minefields and abrupt turns. Now, having made this effort to connect the dots, I see that those twists and turns, including all the stumbling blocks, false hopes, and blind alleys along the way, were really part of a single path, and that my compass always pointed to my true north.

Instead of free-falling or even falling down, I have been continually falling up. For instance, five months after my talk in Austin, when the start-up bank deal evaporated, I went to work for Ernst & Young's cleantech practice, an opportunity I created by working both my network and my ability to turn failure into success. The work with EY continued my focus on advising cleantech company CEOs and bringing them together with corporations and potential strategic partners. Through EY, I got a chance to help many more people tell their stories and build their businesses—a successful pivot from the work I did as a consultant on my own.

Going to EY wasn't a step down or a retreat from my entrepreneurial dreams, rather I was falling up into something that would help me do more with more resources—and simultaneously help me take the leap I needed to make in my life. And over the first two years at EY the work was rewarding, I loved being part of a team that was building something together.

Then, as often happens in big organizations, another unexpected change came my way. Our team, a three-year-old experiment to build a cleantech practice, got swallowed up by the much larger power and utilities group. My boss had lobbied for one final meeting with the decision makers and his supervisor, one opportunity to pitch the value proposition our group provided the firm. For the week or so before the meeting, we accumulated the relevant data-ammunition and loaded it into a PowerPoint deck. He took the meeting on his own and I was anxious for the result.

Samantha and I were just about to fly off for our honeymoon when the email from my boss arrived on my smartphone. "Meeting went well," he wrote. "They're on board. Enjoy your honeymoon." Relieved, I didn't check my email until we returned two weeks later.

When I got back, I learned that, in fact, the meeting hadn't gone well. Our group was done, and further, we were to wind things down by the end of October after our annual cleantech CEO retreat in California, an event I'd managed for the previous two years. None of our team was sure what we would do next. Was I going to be out of a job? I'd just remarried, and we'd bought a house together, blending our family, and started building the life of our dreams— was it all going to come crashing down?

For me, as luck would have it, a meeting with a woman in the firm who now became my manager determined the next phase of my working life. She had other ideas for me, and, for my part, I had another opportunity to tell my story, and to bring my authentic self to the table. Once again, I had a chance to fall up.

A great manager will get to know who you are, not just what you've been doing, and my first conversation with my new manager was about who I was, not about what I'd done at the firm. She wanted to know what made me tick, what passions I had, what about my experience made me unique. I told her about my international work with the Nature Conservancy and the social venture capital organization, Ashoka, and about my work with cleantech CEOs and companies with my own consulting practice prior to joining EY.

Our conversation led to a new assignment that would best use my skills, experience, and passions to benefit both the firm and me. The project was to globalize an innovative new venture launched by our South African practice around smart metering as a managed service.

The sponsoring partner, a U.K.-based Aussie, fully believed in the idea he got tapped with sponsoring, wanted to see it come to fruition, and gave me the resources and authority to push it forward. We spent three years building-out the technology-based smart metering solution, creating a business model and value proposition, getting buy-in throughout the organization, battling for resources, and making it work. It was like running a start-up in a big organization. I was in entrepreneurial heaven.

When, two years into development, we realized we couldn't scale the service alone, we sought a technology partner to help us take it to the next level. I approached the team leaders for several of our firm's technology alliances, settling on Microsoft as the one with the best combination of price-point, capabilities, and brand recognition. The executive team gave us a much-needed injection of cash and adopted the solution as one of the firm's global priorities. We were off and running.

And then, I hit a professional impasse, another precipice on the edge of a chasm. Our sector leader considered my task complete: adopted firm-wide, our solution had garnered buy-in from the executive committee, and regional sales people began selling it through their infrastructure. I'd done what I was asked to do, but now there was nothing left for me at this firm. It was time for me to leave, to disrupt myself. In truth, I was heartbroken. This stimulating and rewarding project that played to my skillsets and allowed me to make a mark, was now being taken away from me. Mortified, I had to find another way to fall up.

*   *   *   *   *

A short time after I left EY, I thought of my old friend and mentor, Harry Groome, and went to see him. When I first met Harry in 1998, he served as a board member of the Nature Conservancy. In that capacity, he had interviewed me for a role with the organization's Pennsylvania chapter and in our first meeting, we learned we shared three passions in addition to conservation: fly-fishing, ice hockey, and writing.

Harry told me that, as a young man, he wanted to be a writer but had put writing aside when he took a job in the early 1960s with the company with whom he spent his entire career, eventually becoming its chairman. Upon retirement, he took up writing again, short stories primarily, got an MFA from Vermont College, and eventually wrote four novels.

A few years later, the Millay Colony offered me a month-long residency and I took a sabbatical from the Conservancy to pursue it. "Someday you're going to have to choose," Harry said to me. "You can't do both—you can't be both a successful writer *and* a successful executive."

In the wake of leaving EY, I turned to my writing again, in earnest, and with a passion I thought I'd lost. During that time, I did some consulting, and even looked at some longer-term executive positions, but I couldn't find a role that got me excited enough to go back into full-time work. I'd lost interest in climbing a corporate ladder and playing in other people's sandboxes.

Then Samantha said to me, "You know, Scott, you're happiest when you're writing." I had to admit the truth in that statement. I'd never fully committed myself to being a writer—not fully. There was always a part of me that wanted to be "successful" in work *outside* of writing. But now I began to realize there are different ways to define success.

Over the months following my departure from EY, I started thinking that perhaps Harry and

Samantha were right. Perhaps the universe was giving me another second chance; it certainly seemed to be sending me messages to that effect: first, a publisher wrote to say she wanted to bring out my book, *Dwelling: an ecopoem*, which I wrote during that long-ago month at the Millay Colony; then, I got invited to participate in a residency on São Miguel Island, in the Azores, to work on a project exploring my family's roots there; and I started working on this little book that's in your hands.

Meanwhile, consulting gigs came and went, a few corporate and non-profit jobs I expressed interest in did not materialize, and my old boss at EY approached me about joining his new team, but even that didn't pan out.

I remember something one of my heroes, the writer Annie Dillard, once said, "How we spend our days is, of course, how we spend our lives." The average person spends over 90,000 hours at work over a lifetime—that's a big chunk of our lives, more than anything we do outside of sleeping. Today, I'm spending most days—or most mornings anyway—writing. Perhaps, now, I can best contribute to changing the world through my writing.

* * * * *

"The first study of the man who wants to be a poet is the knowledge of himself," Rimbaud wrote in his letter, before he prescribes how to become a seer. "He looks for his soul, inspects it, tests it, learns it. As soon as he knows it, he must cultivate it."

It feels, at age fifty-five, that I'm finally spending my days where my journey was taking me all along, cultivating that self-knowledge into something greater than myself. Forty years after my fall at Letchworth Gorge, I'm finally becoming the writer I was meant to be—in a place where I belong, with a partner who wants me to be the "Papa" of my deepest dreams, and I am grateful.

I'm not sure where my path will take me next, but through this exploration of my life of second chances and connecting the dots of my past, I know that I will find my way, I'll continue to fall up. In the end, I now know what matters most to me, how to pursue it, and how to fully embrace it.

WORKS CITED

Bornstein, David. *How to Change the World: Social Entrepreneurs and the Power of New Ideas*. New York: Oxford University Press, 2004.

Dillard, Annie. *The Writing Life*. 1st ed., New York: HarperCollins, 1989.

Gladwell, Malcolm. "Late Bloomers," *The New Yorker*, 13 October 2008.

Jobs, Steve. "Text of Steve Jobs' Commencement Address (2005)." *Stanford News*, 12 June 2005, news.stanford.edu/2005/06/14/jobs-061505/.

Rimbaud, Arthur. "The 'Voyant' *Letter to Paul Demeny*, 1871," translated by Oliver Bernard, in *Toward the Open Field: Poets on the Art of Poetry, 1800-1950*. Edited by Melissa Kwasny. Middletown, CT: Wesleyan Univ. Press, 2004.

ACKNOWLEDGMENTS

I wish to thank the following for their interest and engagement with my writing and the various components of what became this book: L. L. Barkat, who first got me thinking about writing memoir in a substantive way; Simmons Buntin, who published my essay on storytelling as an agent of change in *Terrain* back in 2006; Peter Forbes and Helen Whybrow, whose pioneering work on storytelling and conservation helped catalyze my work in this area with the Pennsylvania Land Trust Association and The Nature Conservancy; Cam Danielson, whose work on conscious leadership has been a thoughtful touchstone for me over the years and whose friendship has been a tremendous gift; Mark Danowsky of *Schuylkill Valley Journal*, who originally asked me to write about Malcolm Gladwell's *Revisionist History* podcast episode "Hallelujah," and the experimental versus conceptual innovator construct as it applies to poetry, but totally embraced what I came back with instead; Alison Hawthorne

Deming, whose friendship has been as constant as her work and example as a poet and essayist; Whitney Johnson and Phyllis Mufson, who both challenged me to live more fully and intentionally—and to never settle for less than one's possibility, even when or especially when it means disrupting yourself; Jack Ricchiuto, who taught me to write a different narrative and whose friendship is more like brotherhood; Robert Michael Pyle, who taught me to look to my own backyard for inspiration and to teach others to care; Kathryn Miles, who helped me find the pivot that led to the thesis this book represents; Lee Kravitz, who helped me uncover the real story hidden in the shadows of my original manuscript; Lucinda Duncalfe, who lent a fresh pair of eyes to the final product and whose conversations over lunch for the past twenty years have always been a beacon of inspiration—even when I left the car running; and, finally, to my editor L. M. Browning for inspiring me to write with radical authenticity, for believing in this work, and for helping shepherd it into what you now hold in your hands.

Several sections of this work originally appeared—in sometimes radically different form—

in *Schuylkill Valley Journal, Terrain.org,* and my blogs *TheGreenSkeptic.com* and *seapoetry.wordpress.com.* I also wish to thank the Millay Colony and Concordia Foundation for time and space to write some of the words that appear in this book, and friends and colleagues from The Nature Conservancy and many other conservation organizations for inspiring me over the years to strive for a world where people and nature thrive. As I relate elsewhere, Gladys Taylor was an early source of inspiration to me and nurtured my lifelong curiosity about the world in ways that helped me become a poet, conservationist, and better human being.

Jasper, Walker, and Elizabeth Anderson and Max, Erica, and Sasha Beinhacker have each helped me see the world differently and to dedicate myself to making the world a better place for them and, someday, for their children—our grandchildren. Calvin and Beverley (and Bonnie long before either of them) have been great canine companions on many trails and city streets.

And, last but certainly not least, this book would not be possible without the love of my life, Samantha, who from our early days as friends to and through our marriage as partners in a blended family and in life, has always wanted me to realize my full potential and become the man I am today.

–SEA
March 2019

About the Author

Scott Edward Anderson is the author of *Dwelling: an ecopoem*, *Fallow Field*, and *Walks in Nature's Empire*. He has been a Concordia Fellow at the Millay Colony for the Arts and received the Nebraska Review Award. His poetry has appeared in *The American Poetry Review*, *Alaska Quarterly Review*, *Cimarron Review*, *The Cortland Review*, *The Wayfarer*, and two anthologies. His essays and reviews have appeared in *basalt*, *The Bloomsbury Review*, *Cleaver*, the *Philadelphia Inquirer*, *Schuylkill Valley Journal*, and elsewhere. For many years, he has worked in conservation, social enterprise, and clean energy consulting with such organizations as The Nature Conservancy, Ashoka, VerdeStrategy, and EY. He lives in Brooklyn, NY, with his wife, Samantha, and their blended family.

WWW.SCOTTEDWARDANDERSON.COM

LITTLE
BOUND BOOKS

THE LITTLE BOUND BOOKS ESSAY SERIES

———

OTHER OFFERINGS IN THE SERIES

To Lose the Madness by L.M. Browning
A Comet's Tail by Amy Nawrocki
A Fistful of Stars by Gail Collins-Ranadive
A Letter to My Daughters by Theodore Richards
Terranexus by David K. Leff
What Comes Next by Heidi Barr
Great Pan is Dead by Eric D. Lehman

WWW.LITTLEBOUNDBOOKS.COM
LOOK FOR OUR TITLES WHEREVER BOOKS ARE SOLD

HOMEBOUND PUBLICATIONS

Ensuring that the mainstream isn't the only stream.

AT HOMEBOUND PUBLICATIONS, we publish books written by independent voices for independent minds. Our books focus on a return to simplicity and balance, connection to the earth and each other, and the search for meaning and authenticity. We strive to ensure that the mainstream is not the only stream. In all our titles, our intention is to introduce new perspectives that will directly aid humankind in the trials we face at present as a global village.

WWW.HOMEBOUNDPUBLICATIONS.COM
LOOK FOR OUR TITLES WHEREVER BOOKS ARE SOLD

SINCE 2011

✳